To Elias,

May you [ ] this book to help you find answers to questions you have. Look up verses in your Bible too.

Emily Learns About Christianity

By John R. Mitchell

our love & prayers,
Grammy & Grampy

Acknowledgements

I want to thank pastors John Starr and Dave Buche for reviewing the doctrinal issues discussed in this book. Their comments were greatly appreciated, and suggestions were incorporated into my writing.

This book is dedicated to my wife, Leslie, who helped me early in our lives to become serious about my faith. God Bless you, my love!

Thank you to Dave Pool, Ernest Dietrich, John Starr, Mike Kirk, Ed Peverelle, and Rodney Nielsen for direction and education in leading a Christian Life.

Cover photo is by Rachael Collins. Thank you.

Index

Chapter 1: Who is God?

A silver van pulled up into the driveway on Grampa and Gramma's farm one Monday morning in June. Their eleven year old granddaughter, Emily, hopped out as soon as the van came to a stop. Emily had come to visit her grandparents for a week. She rushed up to Gramma, hugged and kissed her, and turned to Grampa, giving him a big hug and kiss as well, and pulled out a folded paper and said, "Hello, Grampa! I have a whole list of things I want to do this week! I hope we have time for them."

"Emily, it's good that you can come and stay with us this week. We have a list of things to do, too. Gramma plans to keep you busy, and we hope you have fun during your stay."

Her parents took Emily's suitcase upstairs to the bedroom she would use, and they stayed and visited for several hours, sharing a lunch Gramma had prepared. When it was time to leave, Mom and Dad kissed Emily good-bye and headed home. She promised to call them every

5

evening. After they left, Gramma and Grampa sat down with Emily in the family room to visit some more.

"Now that you are growing up, Em, perhaps you have some questions for us that we can try to answer," said Gramma. "We know you have been attending church, and thought perhaps you might have some questions about what you have heard in your Christian studies. We have a whole week to discuss them, and we have many things you can help with here on the farm."

"Yes, I do, Gramma. I'm not sure where to start right now. Let me think about it some."

They were sitting in their family room, and Grampa turned on the television. Emily loved baseball, and they tuned in a game to watch her favorite team play.

After the first scoreless inning was over, Emily turned to her grandmother with a question.

"Gramma. I've been learning about God in church, but there are some things I don't understand. What can you tell me about Him?"

"God is our Heavenly Father," said Gramma. "He is the Lord of Lords, and the King of kings, Creator of all things, and Master of the

Universe. He is the One we pray to, and He answers our prayers. He created the earth and everything that lives here. What else would you like to know about Him?"

Emily thought for a moment.

"Gramma, that's quite a list of names for God. How do you know all this?"

Gramma walked over to a bookshelf, picked up a book, and brought it to the couch where Emily was sitting next to Grampa.

"All that and more is in this Bible, which Grampa and I bought especially for you. This is our present to you, Emily."

Emily took the book and looked it over. "Oh! This is wonderful, thanks! My first Bible!"

"This will tell you all about God and Jesus," said Gramma. She opened the book for Emily and began to go through it with her.

"The first section is called the Old Testament. It is the story of Earth's beginnings, the creation of man, and the story of the Hebrew nation. They were called God's Chosen People. It is filled with history, God's laws, and the prophesies of things to come. You may have heard stories of Adam and Eve, Noah, Moses,

Abraham, David and Goliath, and Jonah and the whale. These stories are all in the Old Testament, along with many other important historical stories.

"The second section of the Bible is called the New Testament. It covers the life of Jesus, the selection and works of the Apostles, and the spread of Christianity. It contains many teachings of Jesus, and letters from His disciples. And, even though it was written a long time ago, it is still read and studied by us today. It speaks to Grampa and me every time we open its pages."

"What do you mean, 'it speaks to you?' How can a book speak?"

Grampa chuckled, then said, "What Gramma is saying is that every time we read a portion of it, we learn something, even though we have read many of these passages often. The Bible is also called 'the Living Word' because, even though it was written nearly two thousand years ago, it is still important today. It is still fresh and exciting. It is our instruction manual for our lives."

Emily turned to the table of contents.

"We have talked about it in Sunday school class, and our teacher has read some stories from it for us. Wow! There are lots of chapters in here. Who wrote the Bible?"

Gramma smiled and said, "There were many people who wrote this book over many thousands of years. Their letters and stories are referred to as books within the Bible. Their works were combined into this one book. God is the author of this, through the writings of His people. He told them what to write; He 'inspired' them. Later, Bible scholars assembled them into the Bible that we have today."

"It took thousands of years to write this? Wow! And, some of these titles I can't even pronounce. Like this one. D-e-u-t-e-r-o-..."

"That's Deuteronomy," interrupted Grampa. "Before you leave, we'll help you pronounce all the books of the Bible. Don't worry, you'll learn them all in time."

"Here's an easy one. Daniel. What's that book all about?"

Gramma smiled warmly. "That book is one of my favorites. It's a story about the Hebrew nation during their exile, when they were ruled by the nation of Babylon. The Babylonians took the Hebrews as slaves and mistreated them. Daniel rose up as a prophet and leader of the exiles to show the Babylonian king who the true God was, and to overcome the bad treatment the Hebrews were receiving. It has lots of prophesy in it, too. It's a wonderful story of God's love and Daniel's faithfulness to God, no matter what his circumstances were."

"Have you ever seen God?"

Gramma chuckled. "No, dear, we have never seen Him physically, but we know He exists. We see his handiwork every day, in all He created. We even see Him in you."

"Yes, Emily," said Grampa, "We see him in the animals and plants He created, in the sunshine and rain He brings us, in the beautiful sunsets He gives us in the evening. I think about God every time I pick a tomato from the garden, or take a bite of Gramma's apple pie.

"God was the creator of everything. He created the Earth that we live on, the sky above us, the air that we breath, the sun and rain, the water we drink and bathe with, the food we eat and everything around us. Isaiah 6 says, '*the earth is filled with His glory'*"

"God has many more names and titles in the Bible," proclaimed Gramma, "including Holy of Holies, the Great I Am, and Father to all."

"What other questions do you have about God?" asked Grampa.

"Where did God come from?"

"God is eternal," said Gramma, "and we are told that He was here to create the heavens and the earth. Genesis begins with *'In the beginning, God...'* We don't know where He came from or when, but He is eternal."

"I think you both have answered my questions so far, but I'm sure I will have more," Emily said.

They continued watching the ball game, and Emily looked through her Bible, reading here and there until the game ended and it was dinnertime. After dinner, Grampa excused himself to finish some evening chores. Emily called home to tell her parents about her gift, and then went outside to help him if she could.

11

Chapter 2: Where did the Earth come from?

The next morning, Grampa was working in his garden before breakfast, when Emily came outside.

"Gramma said breakfast will be ready in 15 minutes. What are you working on this morning? Can I help?"

"Yes. Thank you for asking, Emily. That's really sweet of you. I'm setting out some of my tomato plants. I've dug holes for the plants, and if you would hand those eight plants to me, I'll put them in the ground. We have some nice rich soil here, and we should have some nice ripe tomatoes in a few months. Would you hand me two of them?"

Emily picked up two tomato plants and handed them to Grampa.

"I read some of my Bible last night. I started at the beginning, in Genesis. Grampa, where did the Earth come from? I read that God created it, but in science class, my teacher told us about a Big Bang, where all the planets came from one massive ball exploding. I don't know who is right."

Grampa mounded dirt up around the tomato plants, then turned to his granddaughter.

"Scientists have theories about how the Earth came into existence; the most popular one of which is the Big Bang Theory. They believe that there was this huge mass of dirt and rock which exploded, and from this all the suns, planets, moons, asteroids, meteors, comets, and other spacial objects came into existence. Mind you, it is only a theory; a scientific guess, about the origins of the Universe. However, scientists don't know where this one big mass of dirt and rock came from, or how it came to explode. Where did space come from? Where did the energy come from to cause this massive explosion?

"In Genesis, we read about how God, the creator of the universe, did it. We believe the biblical creation over this 'accident' the scientists call the Big Bang. We are told in Genesis that God can create something from nothing. Science says we can't do that."

"Okay, Grampa, but how did God create the Earth?"

"We aren't told the details of the creation

except what we were given in the first chapters of Genesis. What we are told here is that God created this huge ball of dirt and rock we call Earth, then He created a sun to provide us with heat and light for the Earth. Next, He created other planets and the Earth's Moon. After He created Earth, he graced our planet with water and oxygen, along with carbon dioxide, nitrogen and other gases, so we could have an atmosphere. Next, He created vast oceans and rivers. And so with all this, the Earth could support life.

"Plants were the first to be created, followed by the fish of the sea, the birds of the air, and all the animals on land and sea.

"We breathe in oxygen, and breathe out carbon dioxide. These tomato plants take in carbon dioxide and give off oxygen. They need nitrogen and other nutrients, as well as sunlight and water, to grow. This is a miracle in itself; that God had this idea for life on Earth.

"And, His final creation was the best of all. He created..."

"Mankind!" Emily finished his statement.

"You are right, Emily!" Grampa laughed

and opened his Bible. "Genesis 1:27 reads, *So God created man in his own image, in the image of God he created him; male and female he created them.* And going to Genesis 2, starting with verse 21, *So the LORD God caused a deep sleep to fall upon the man, and while he slept took one of his ribs and closed up its place with flesh. And the rib that the LORD God had taken from the man he made into a woman and brought her to the man. Then the man said, 'This at last is bone of my bones and flesh of my flesh; she shall be called Woman, because she was taken out of Man.' Therefore a man shall leave his father and his mother and hold fast to his wife, and they shall become one flesh.* The woman was created to be the wife and helpmate of the man. They are to love and cherish one another. And, with the creation of Adam and Eve, God's creation was complete, and He called it 'Good.' As companions in life, husband and wife need to work together as a team, and learn to love one another more and more, so they can grow together in everything that is good."

"So, every time I see a plant, an animal or a person, I see God's creation, right?" asked

Emily.

"That's exactly right, Emily. God's handiwork can be seen in every living thing, whether it is a plant or animal, insect or bird. It can be seen in the mountains and the deserts. Every time it rains, I think of God. The sun, moon, stars, even the wind that blows shows us a God who planned all this."

"What about the river that runs through the back of your farm?"

"Yes, that river is God's creation, too. He created the creeks, rivers, lakes and oceans. All living things need water. None of the other planets in our solar system have water that we know of. Scientists have not yet found any evidence of life on any other planets. Only Earth can support life as we know it."

They had finished planting the tomatoes by now, so Grampa and Emily headed into the house to wash up for breakfast. Gramma had prepared bacon and eggs, along with a plate of sliced tomatos she had bought at the store.

"Yum! I love tomatoes! Grampa and I were just planting some of these," she announced to Gramma. "Did you know God created them?"

"Oh, yes. God created them, Grampa plants them and cares for them, and I harvest them when they are ripe. Isn't God good?" Gramma asked.

"He's the best!" Emily nodded. "Pass me God's tomatoes, please."

Chapter 3 Who is the Holy Spirit?

Later that day, Gramma, Grampa and Emily were relaxing and reading in their family room. A gentle rain was now falling outside. Emily was intent on reading her new Bible when suddenly she stopped with a curious expression on her face.

"Gramma, what can you tell me about the Holy Spirit? What is it? I've been reading about it in my Bible."

"Well, Emily, the Holy Spirit is an interesting subject," Gramma responded. "First of all, the Holy Spirit is a person, not an 'it,' and part of the Trinity. He is God in one of His three forms."

"The Spirit enters us when we decide to

give our lives to Jesus and are baptized. Before that, He works on us. We become Christians, and promise to live by God's laws," Grampa said. "That's why it's important to study the Bible, which is God's word to live by. The more we know God's word, the better off we are. It is very important to know how God wants us to live our lives."

"Some people say the Holy Spirit is your conscience, but He is more than that," Gramma interjected. "The Bible tells us the Holy Spirit lives in us and guides us. It's referred to as indwelling. He helps you know what is right and what is wrong. It's like when you want a cookie, but Mom tells you 'No'. You've been taught that stealing is wrong. Yet, you want to snitch one, but inside something tells you not to disobey your mother. The Holy Spirit does that and more, like letting you know there are other things you should not do, and some things you should do; such as helping others. You may have heard people say, 'What would Jesus do?' The more you read and understand His word, the better Christian life you can live."

"Another thing He does," Grampa

continued, "is to help us when we tell others about our faith. Sometimes He puts words in our mouths. He also warns us of sinful things and tries to help us steer clear of sin."

"So, how do I know He is living in me? Does He really speak to me?"

"He is silent, but speaks through your subconscious. And sometimes He speaks to us through other people. The scriptures talk about the fruit of the Spirit being love, joy, peace, patience, kindness, goodness, faithfulness, gentleness and self-control. If you live by the Spirit, you will experience these fruits."

"Fruits? What are you talking about, Grampa?"

"We could call them gifts, too. When we plant and care for an apple tree, it produces gifts for us in the form of its fruit, apples. The Spirit's fruit is nothing we can eat, but is given to us to make our lives full. I remember the joy your mother had when you were born. She was so happy, and gave you all the care and love she knew how to give, and that joy never goes away if she continues to live in Christ."

"Do you and Gramma live in Christ?"

"We try our best to live our lives the way God wants us to, just like your parents do, but sometimes we go against God's word. That is known as sin, and we are guilty of it the same as everyone on Earth is. No one is perfect. We all fall short of God's desires."

"What happens when we sin?"

"God is not pleased with sin. We disappoint Him, like when you disobey your parents. But He loves us anyway. That's where Jesus comes in. He is our savior. We confess our sins to God, and He forgives us. He also expects us to repent from those sins."

"What's that word mean? How do we repent? Pastor Dave has talked about it in some of his sermons on Sunday."

"Repenting means to change our ways. We turn from doing wrong to doing right," said Gramma. "If we are mean to someone, we need to replace that meanness with kindness. This is very important to God.

"Do you remember the story about Peter denying he was friends with Jesus three times after Jesus was arrested? Peter lied to the people he talked to. But Jesus forgave him for each of those three times. Peter never again denied that he knew Jesus."

"The Holy Spirit helped him tell others about the good news of Jesus," Grampa said. "Jesus's death, and His defeat of death when He rose again from the tomb three days later is the best miracle of all. This is what Christianity is all about.

"Now, young lady, I think it's bedtime. You need to call your parents, and then we can say our prayers. We will have much more to talk about tomorrow."

Chapter 4 Who is Jesus?

The next morning, when Grampa came in from his morning chores, he found Emily at the kitchen table, reading her Bible.

"Good morning, Em. What are you reading about?"

"I'm reading the Book of Luke in the New Testament. He wrote about Jesus. We talked about Him quite a lot yesterday and last Sunday in Sunday school class. But there is much I still don't understand about Him. I know we celebrate His birthday at Christmas. I know the Christmas story. I played the part of an angel in a play we did at church. I'm hoping Luke will help me know more about Him."

"Luke is a wonderful book to read about Jesus," said Gramma as she entered the kitchen. "What would you like to know?"

"I know He is God from discussions we had in Sunday School, but why was He born and why did He come to Earth from Heaven? What was His purpose?"

" Over two thousand years ago," Gramma began, "a baby was born who would change the world. He was born to a woman named Mary and her husband Joseph. They were selected by God to be His earthly parents. Jesus is the Savior who God sent to bring a new message of salvation and hope into the world. He came to find those lost to God and to lead them to salvation. He is the Messiah the Old Testament tells us about. There are over forty prophecies in the Old Testament books about the Messiah, and Jesus fulfilled every one of them."

"What is salvation?" asked Emily.

Grampa answered with a smile. "We believe all people have a soul. When we die, our soul lives on eternally. It's called eternal life. Now, if we receive salvation from God, we will live forever with Him in Heaven. If we do not receive salvation, we will live forever apart from Him. Jesus came to Earth to tell us about salvation and show us how to receive it. Jesus came to save sinners."

"So how do we earn salvation?"

"Oh no, dear, we cannot earn salvation," Gramma replied. "Salvation is freely given to us through Jesus. All we need to do is claim it. And your next question is, how do we do that, right?"

"How did you know that, Gramma?"

"To claim salvation, we need to confess our sins, repent of them, and accept Jesus as our savior. It sounds simple, right?"

"Okay, it does sound simple, but let's start from the beginning. You used a lot of words I don't understand."

"All right," said Grampa, "We'll start from the beginning. Do you understand what sin is?"

"Sin is doing something wrong, and not doing what is right," Emily replied. "We talked about that yesterday."

"Yes. That's a good start. Sin is doing something wrong in God's eyes. It doesn't mean only robbery or murder; it can include disobedience to your parents, bullying someone else, cheating on a test in school, lying to others, or even not doing our chores. Taking the Lord's name in vain is a common sin. And, sin separates us from God.

"To confess our sins, we need to understand what our sins are and then we must confess them to God. Usually we do this in prayer to Him.

"Our next step is to repent of our sins, and we talked briefly about that yesterday as well. That means we stop doing those wrong things. For instance, if one of our sins is disobeying our parents, we take steps to obey them at all times."

"Always?" asked Emily.

"Yes, dear, always!" said Gramma. "I know it's hard to do sometimes, but we must do this the best that we know how."

Emily hung her head for a moment, and then asked, "What if we are trying to do good, but do some wrong things instead?"

"Then we ask for forgiveness and try not to do those things again. And, if we have done something wrong to another person, it's important to sincerely apologize for that wrong, and make it right. You see, Emily, not one of us is perfect, the way God is. We all sin and fall short of what God expects of us. Even the Apostle Paul writes about how he sins and doesn't meet God's expectations."

"Accepting Jesus as our savior is a very important step in our salvation," said Grampa.

"Paul considered himself a sinner? But he ministered to so many people, and seemed like a very Godly man."

"He was all that, but he knew he was not perfect, and therefore considered himself a sinner. He was a mortal man, just like us, and he wrote much of the new testament for us to study," Grampa stated. "He was a very special one of God's workers, but he was a sinner too. He even tells us this in his letters."

"I thought I'd show you how to do some counted cross stitch after church today, Emily." Gramma proposed. "Would you be interested in learning this?

"That sounds wonderful, Gramma. I'm ready to start!"

Chapter 5 What is the Resurrection all about?

At lunch that day, Emily had some new questions for her grandparents.

"Last Easter, we talked in church about Jesus's death on the cross. That seems like a terrible way to die! And, the minister told us about His resurrection. I'd like to know more."

"You are right about His death on the cross," exclaimed Gramma. "That was a Roman way of punishing evil doers for their crimes. They wanted to make examples of this cruel death to discourage other people from committing crimes."

"But Jesus wasn't bad, was He?"

"No, Emily, He was not evil, nor was He a criminal. He was a sinless, innocent and perfect man in every way," Grampa responded.

"Then, I don't understand why they killed Him."

"There were leaders of the Jewish church

who believed the message He was teaching was blasphemous. That means it went against what they believed or what they were taught. They did not believe He was the Messiah, the Son of God, and they were not ready to accept His message of salvation. They didn't really listen to Him or even understand His message. They felt He was not able to forgive people of their sin. They believed that only God could do this, and this man named Jesus was not God in their eyes; He was merely a carpenter's son who knew enough of the scriptures to quote them. So they had Him arrested and taken before the Roman authorities, who would put Him to death.

"But they also didn't understand the old testament prophecies that He would rise from the dead on the third day. So, when they found the stone of the tomb rolled away, and Jesus's body was gone, they accused His followers of opening the tomb and stealing His body."

"That could not happen, though, because Roman soldiers had been posted at the tomb to prevent anything like this from happening. Also, the stone sealing the entrance to the tomb was extremely heavy; too heavy for the Apostles to move. The guards knew that they would face the death penalty if anyone broke into the tomb and stole the body.

"The Jewish leaders told everyone that He was dead and His followers had stolen the body. But His body was never found, because Jesus had risen. The scriptures record numerous appearances He made with the Apostles and other believers before He ascended into Heaven. Jesus appeared before more than five hundred people after He rose from the grave."

"Thank you, Gramma, for explaining that to me. I understand why Easter is so important to our church."

"It is very important to every Christian worldwide," said Grampa. "Had He not risen from the grave, we would not call Him the Messiah, and Christianity would not exist. We would have no stories of Jesus or the Apostles. There would be no New Testament. We would be worshiping God the same way the Hebrews of the Old Testament did.

"Jesus takes away the penalty of death and the grave so we can live forever. Our physical death is only temporary."

"Can you give me some examples of ancient prophecies that came true?" Emily asked.

"How about turning to Isaiah 53:3-9 and read that to me," Grampa asked.

Emily opened her Bible to the chapter Grampa called for, and read the following: *He was despised and rejected by men, a man of sorrows and acquainted with grief; and as one from whom men hide their faces He was despised, and we esteemed Him not. Surely He has borne our griefs and carried our sorrows; yet we esteemed Him stricken, smitten by God, and afflicted. But He was pierced for our transgressions; He was crushed for our iniquities; upon h\Him was the chastisement that brought us peace, and with His wounds we are healed. All we like sheep have gone astray; we have turned—every one—to His own way; and the Lord has laid on Him the iniquity of us all. He was oppressed, and He was afflicted, yet He opened not His mouth; like a lamb that is led to the slaughter, and like a sheep that before its shearers is silent, so He opened not his mouth. By oppression and judgment He was taken away; and as for His generation, who considered that*

He was cut off out of the land of the living, stricken for the transgression of my people? And they made His grave with the wicked and with a rich man in His death, although He had done no violence, and there was no deceit in His mouth.

"Gee, Grampa, I don't understand all of what I read, but much of this seems to be about the death of Jesus, right?"

"Yes, Emily, that's what it is all about. And this was written nearly 800 years before Jesus was born."

"Wow! How did Isaiah know this would come about?" Emily asked.

"He wrote what God inspired him to write, dear. He undoubtedly had no idea what the prophecy he was writing referred to, but he followed God's instructions to write this all down."

"I wonder if Isaiah was scratching his head after he wrote this," Emily said.

"Yes, I imagine he was very puzzled with this chapter.

"Now I believe we have some chickens to attend to, and some eggs to gather for Gramma. And after that, I've got a Slip 'n' Slide I can put on that small hill in the back yard, and you can go sliding."

Chapter 6 Is the Bible True?

That evening, Emily, Gramma and Grampa were sitting in the living room. Although the television was on, Emily was intently reading her Bible. Suddenly, she raised her head and looked at Gramma.

"How do we know the Bible is true, Gramma? Don't some people say it isn't true, and that the stories in it are just made up?"

Gramma and Grampa were silent for a moment, and then Grampa spoke up.

"That's a good question, Em. The Bible is our primary source of information about Jesus, His life, and His teachings. It's the cornerstone piece of literature for the Christian faith, and all Chrisianity is based upon the truth of this document.

"Truth must be tested through observation, scientific evidence, experimentation, examination and eyewitness testimony. We have the Apostles and thousands of believers, such as Luke, Peter, Titus, Timothy and Stephen, who lived in the time of Jesus; some even traveled with Him. The Apostle Paul, who wrote many of the letters in the New Testament, gave his life, as did all the others, to preach the Gospel of Jesus."

"I read where the apostle Thomas actually touched the hands of Jesus after the resurrection. Is that true, Grampa?" Emily asked.

"Yes, Emily. That is true. You are referring to the book of John 20 verses 25- 27. Thomas was not with the other apostles when Jesus appeared to them, so when they told him that Jesus was alive, he refused to believe them. He said, *'Unless I see in his hands the mark of the nails, and place my finger into the mark of the nails, and place my hand into his side, I will never believe.'* This was totally unbelievable to Thomas that Jesus was alive. He had seen Him put to death on the cross and sealed in the tomb. And, as we continue to read from verse 28, *Eight days later, His disciples were inside again, and Thomas was with them. Although the doors were locked, Jesus came and stood among them and said, 'Peace be with you.' Then He said to*

Thomas, *'Put your finger here, and see my hands; and put out your hand, and place it in my side. Do not disbelieve, but believe.' Thomas answered him, 'My Lord and my God!' Jesus said to him, 'Have you believed because you have seen me? Blessed are those who have not seen and yet have believed.'*

"This was an eye-witness account of Jesus's resurrection. Thomas actually touched His wounds. Thomas goes from a person of doubt to a man who confirms that Jesus is God.

"We have very accurate historical data written by ancient historians such as Josephus and Tacitus, who recorded information about Jesus. As historians, they are required to record factual history as accurately as possible. Neither of these men were Christians, nor did they believe in Jesus. The gospels were written within a close amount of time of their recorded events and during the time these eye witnesses or their close family members were still living.

"Over five hundred people saw Him after the resurrection and before He ascended into Heaven.

"We have more historical data recorded

33

through the many prophecies and the fulfillment of these prophecies. Verification of many historic accounts recorded in the old testament have taken place. One researcher has verified over 80 facts in the book of Acts alone as being true. We have found thousands of historical artifacts and numerous sites we have unearthed that confirm the existence of many Biblical stories and accounts. "

"So, if someone tells me the Bible is full of made-up stories, I can tell them they're wrong, Grampa?"

"Yes. You can politely tell them these stories are all true, that they are recorded history, not made-up fairy tales."

Chapter 7: Who are Muslims and what is the Trinity?

That afternoon, Emily and Grandpa went to town for an ice cream sundae. They placed their order for hot fudge with nuts and whipped cream at the ice cream parlor. When their order came up, they moved to the outdoor patio. It was a nice summer day, and they found a table in the shade. Another couple in their early twenties left the patio as Emily chose a table.

"Grampa, I have a friend from school whose name is Sanaz, and she came from Iran. She says she's a Muslim. What's a Muslim?" asked Emily.

Grampa wiped his mouth with his napkin before he spoke. "A Muslim is a follower of the religion known as Islam. A man by the name of Muhammad lived many years ago, and is considered a very wise prophet by many people. He was born in the year 570, and died in 632. The Muslims call him the founder of the Islamic religion. Why do you ask?"

"She says they worship only one God, Allah, in their temple, not three the way Christians do."

"Emily, many people, even Christians, don't understand the idea of The Holy Trinity, which consists of The Father, The Son, and The Holy Spirit. We talked about the Holy Spirit a couple of days ago. Our God is only one God, but in three persons. That's where the word

Trinity comes from."

"Grampa, I don't understand. How can one God be three persons?"

"That is a difficult concept, and you shouldn't feel bad about not understanding it. Many people are confused by this idea. We don't have anything else to compare it to here on Earth. But perhaps I can help you understand this a little better with a close example.

"Let's say that Gramma puts a skillet on the stove, and when it gets red hot, she drops an ice cube into it. What happens to the ice cube?"

"It melts," Emily responded.

"Right. It becomes water. And what happens to the water?"

Emily thought for a moment, the smiled. "It boils."

"Right again. And when it boils, it changes into steam. Now, if the pan is very hot when the ice cube is dropped into it, it melts and turns to steam very quickly. So, we have steam, water, and ice all at the same time. Water in three forms.

"That's like the Trinity. One God in three forms. Does that help you understand a little better?"

"Oh, some, but I am still confused."

"Let's look at it another way. Let'a take your father, for instance. He is your father, he is my son, and he is your aunt Patty's brother. He is the same one person, but he is three persons in different ways to you, me and Aunt Patty. Does that help you?"

"Yeah. I think that does. Daddy is one person, but different in three ways."

"I think you got it! Emily, you are one smart cookie! Perhaps you can explain this to your Muslim friend so she can understand Christianity better. We have one God, the same as she does, but we worship him in three different ways.

"The Muslims believe there is one god, Allah. They believe Christians believe in three gods; The Almighty God, Jesus, and Mother Mary, who is the mother of Jesus. They don't understand the idea of the Trinity the way we do.

"The Muslims say that America calls herself a Christian nation, but they see all the sin and corruption occurring inside our borders. Many of them call America 'the Great Satan.'

They don't like much of our popular music, our television shows, our movies, our lifestyles and certainly not very much of the music and books we publish. They consider the American way of life perverted."

"Aren't they correct, Grampa?"

"Yes, in many ways they are. Our nation has drifted away from being the Godly nation that our forefathers envisioned when they established the United States of America. Our schools have been forced to discontinue teaching about God and Jesus. But when they took Christianity out of the schools, there was nothing to replace it with. Our nation has embraced many ideas today that are sinful in God's eyes. I am sad that this has happened, and I pray daily for our schools, our nation and its leaders."

Chapter 8: Did we evolve from apes?

After they returned from town, Emily went out to the garden to help Grampa. They pulled a few weeds, and Grampa showed her how to hoe around his plants without damaging them.

"Grampa, you showed me some of the differences between the veggies and weeds that grow in your garden. Where did all these plants come from?"

"Well, Emily, nearly all of them came from seeds, either ones I planted or from other plants growing in the garden. Some of these plants I bought at a store had already been started from seeds."

"That's not exactly what I mean, Grampa. Where did they originally come from? In science class, we studied about evolution. And our books said all plants and animals evolved from a single cell millions of years ago. But the Bible says in Genesis that God created all the animals and plants. Which is correct?"

"Oh, yes, Emily. You've asked a interesting question. Evolutionists believe that all life on our planet evolved from one cell, both plants and animals. They once thought that a number of chemicals were accidentally mixed together, struck by lightning, and became a living cell. Now, their latest theory is that a meteorite brought a living cell or cells to earth, and life as we know it began from that. They claim that plants and animals, as well as bacteria and viruses, all evolved from this one cell. But I don't believe that. We have not discovered life on any planets in our solar system. And, for life to exist inside a meteorite, it would have to live for thousands or millions of years in space free of any atmosphere, food and water, and then survive the extreme high temperatures it would be exposed to when it enters our atmosphere.

"Emily, what would make a pear tree decide all of a sudden to start producing peaches? How could a thistle decide it would grow into an oak tree? How could a lily pad leave the water and become a potato plant? Evolutionists believe this is possible, but have no explanation for how it happened.

"Evolutionists won't accept the idea that life came about through Intelligent Design. They refuse to accept a Creator. They see all life on earth as accidental in origin, with no purpose. But that's not according to God's word. Everything on earth has a purpose, or God would not have created it."

"That idea of evolution sounds creepy, Grampa. I don't understand how scientists can think we evolved from pond slime."

"We are told in Genesis all about the creation of the world and all life, starting with plants, the fish in the sea, the birds in the air, and the animals on land and in the waters of our world. God's final creation was man, which we talked about a few days ago. Science has confirmed that the biblical account of the creation of life happened in the order it is recorded in Genesis, according to the fossil records they have found. The writer of Genesis had no idea that science could prove him to be correct. He wrote what God inspired him to write.

"But there are major problems with the theory of evolution. Science cannot prove higher life forms evolved from lower life forms, because they have no evidence of this. A theory is a guess, with or without evidence to back it up. They say that fish evolved from other life forms like worms that lived in the water. They say that frogs and lizards evolved from fish, which grew legs and lungs and crawled out of the seas to live on land. They say that warm-blooded mammals such as mice and rats evolved from cold-blooded reptiles and amphibians. They believe that birds evolved from ancient reptiles or dinosaurs.

"Let's talk about insects for a moment. Did you know, Emily, that there are over 950,000 different species of insects in the world? Why are there so many varieties?

"God had a purpose for each insect He created. Some insects are beneficial to mankind, such as bees, which pollinate plants and produce honey. Other insects are harmful to us. But many creatures, such as fish, birds and bats, eat insects as food.

"A month ago, the fireflies made their appearance. I know they are one of your favorite insects. How did they evolve so they could produce light? Did some fly decide he wanted to evolve into a firefly and suddenly produce light? Scientists cannot answer that question. And, **why** do they produce light? Scientists believe the light is used to attract the females of their species. But many scientists don't see the hand of Intelligent Design in this creation.

"What would make a frog decide he wanted to become a mammal, such as a mouse? Why would a dog decide he wanted to evolve into a cow? These things just don't happen!

"Certain flowers have very deep centers that only insects and birds, such as the hummingbird, can access for their nectar. Many scientists refuse to see the incredible Intelligent Design, the symbiosis between the flowers, insects, mammals and birds. They call this 'Nature,' and miss God's purpose for His creations."

"Wow, Grampa, I never thought about these things! How would spiders know to spin webs in order to catch insects?"

"That's an excellent example of Intelligent Design, Emily. Most plants rely on hummingbirds, bats, bees and other insects to carry pollen from flower to flower to pollinate them. How do the plants know this will be done? Fruit, berries and nut trees and shrubs rely on animals and birds to eat what they produce and carry away their seeds for new plants to sprout. These are all examples of Intelligent Design."

"You call it 'Intelligent Design,' Grampa, but isn't that God's design?"

"Yes, Emily, that is exactly what it is. God's Intelligent Design. And science cannot explain where this comes from. Did you know that when the Monarch butterflies migrate north in the Spring, that by Fall it's a fourth generation of these butterflies that head south for the winter? How do they know where to go, and when? Scientists call this instinct. Christians know this is God's Intelligent Design.

"Have you ever seen the hummingbirds fattening up in the fall for their flight south across the Gulf of Mexico to South America for the winter? How do they know they need to do this?"

"Gosh, Grampa! I see why you and Gramma enjoy the outdoors and nature as much as you do. You told me you can see God everywhere, and now I see Him too!"

"That's right, Emily. We see God's handiwork everywhere we look."

"So, my next question, did we evolve from apes, is answered, right?"

"Based on our discussion, what do you think?"

"Grampa, the answer is, 'No!' We were created by God. We did not evolve from apes or pond slime, or from a living cell from outer space!"

"Charles Darwin believed in evolution because he found similarities in animals," said Grampa. "But he was wrong. He dismissed the possibility of a Creator. He called evolution a theory, and nothing more. He even questioned why there weren't any fossils of transitional species of animals. We haven't found any, simply because there aren't any."

"Thank you, Grampa, for explaining this to me."

"You're welcome. Now, Emily, I think there is some lemonade in the fridge with our names on it. Do you think we can find it?"

"I'm ready for some. Let's go!"

Chapter 9 Does the Bible mention dinosaurs?

The next morning, when Emily came downstairs for breakfast, Gramma was busy in the kitchen preparing the food.

"Blueberry pancakes are the specialty this morning," she said. "There's milk and orange juice in the fridge. Now, you had a list of things you wanted to do this week. What would you like to do today?"

"Could we go fishing in the river in the back field today?" Emily asked.

Grampa chuckled as he came into the kitchen. "I'm sure we can find time today. You know that's one of my favorite things to do, right?"

"Yes, Grampa. That's why I wanted to do it."

As they ate breakfast, Emily told them she had some more questions.

"I read several chapters of Genesis, about the Creation, and I was wondering about something. It doesn't mention the dinosaurs. Where did they come from?"

"Well," Grampa began, "dinosaurs aren't mentioned because they may have all died off before Adam inhabited the earth. Some scholars believe, though, that some species of dinosaurs did roam the earth when men were created.

"The early Hebrew language didn't have a word for dinosaur, and most of the Hebrews never knew they even existed. There is mention several times in the scriptures the word

46

'behemoth' and that may be a reference to these creatures."

"But Grampa, scientists say these fossils are millions of years old, and Genesis says that animals were all created in a day. Which is right?"

"That's one question people have been arguing about ever since the first dinosaur fossils were discovered in the 1800's. The Bible doesn't tell us. Did God create our solar system, the Earth, and everything that walks, crawls, swims or flies in six earth days, or did it take Him millions of years?

"There are many Christians who believe God actually did this all in six days, like the Bible says. After all, God can do anything, right? But there are other Christians who believe it took Him much longer. John writes in the book of Revelation that to God, a day is like a thousand years, and a thousand years is but a day. And 'thousand' means a very long time to the original writer, because the Hebrews did not have numbers larger than thousand, such as 'million' or 'billion.' To answer your question, we do not know and we're not told by the Biblical authors.

What I do believe is that God created all creatures, dinosaurs included. Did He allow them all to die before He created man? Apparently so. Was He experimenting with them, and decided they were too ferocious for humans to deal with? Again, we do not know, but I will ask Him someday when I get to Heaven.

"Now, Emily, I think it's time for us to go fishing."

Chapter 10 Why do bad things happen to good people?

When Emily and Grampa returned from fishing in the river, Gramma had a good lunch fixed for them.

"We are having chicken noodle soup and ham sandwiches for lunch today. How was fishing?"

"I caught four brook trout, and Grampa caught three. I caught the biggest one, too."

After cleaning up, they sat down for lunch.

"Grampa," asked Emily, "I have another question. Why do bad things happen to good people?"

Grampa thought for a few moments, then said, "Are you asking, 'why does God let bad things happen to people?'

"This is a question we ask God sometimes when we don't understand, usually when we are experiencing pain or suffering in our lives. Sometimes it's when we have our feelings hurt, sometimes when we have a physical problem or illness, or perhaps being falsely accused or blamed for something we didn't do. Often we question God when we suffer losses of possessions or property.

"It might even be the sudden loss of a loved one. We ask, 'Why would God allow this to happen? Why would God allow this loved one, especially someone who is a Christian, to die?' You see, Emily, from God's view, that life is not lost. God is able to restore to that person their life in Heaven, so no loss is suffered on their part. Life is not lost to Him who can restore it.

"But what about the grief that we, the family, experience? When we lose someone, God wants us to feel His strength, His comfort, and His sustaining love during our time of grief.

"But there are some, perhaps many, who wonder how a loving God could allow this person to die.

"This is a hard question to answer. But we must remember, God doesn't promise us a long and prosperous life on earth when we become a Christian. But He does promise us a future eternal life with Him in Heaven."

"But God allows people to die and evil to exist in the world. Why?"

"When God gives his creations life, they all will eventually die. Some creations live only a few days, such as adult flies. Others, such as the tortoise, live over a hundred years on average.

"We may not always understand why a certain tragedy happens, but we know Who will carry us through it," said Grampa. "Many times, something bad can become something good if we wait long enough.

"You remember the story of Joseph and the coat of many colors in the Old Testament, right?"

"Oh, yes. His brothers sold him as a slave, and they told their father that he had died."

"Once Joseph was a slave to a rich man,

and then became a prisoner and was thrown in jail because he was accused of something wrong he had not done. There, he interpreted a dream for the pharaoh's wine taster. Two years later, the pharaoh had some dreams he couldn't interpret, and the wine taster remembered Joseph, still a prisoner. Joseph told the pharaoh that the dreams meant, that there would be seven years of prosperity, followed by seven years of famine. In response to this, the pharaoh elevated Joseph to be in charge of his storehouse and prepare for the famine that was coming. Joseph went from a shepherd, a slave, and a prisoner to the second most powerful man in Egypt. Eventually, he was able to save the pharoah's people and the rest of his family from starvation."

"So, God made something good out of something that started out as a disaster," said Emily.

"You are exactly right," Gramma said. "God made something good out of something bad.

"When something bad happens to us, we so often want to know 'why did this happen?' and we ask God for answers. Occasionally we get our answer quickly, but often it takes time, sometimes years, before the 'why?' is answered. We need to be patient, trust God and not blame Him for our problems and not turn away from Him."

"About the evil in life," Grampa interjected, "someone once told me that God allowed pain in our lives so we could appreciate pleasure so much more. Perhaps evil is here so we can appreciate goodness, kindness and love. That's not in the Bible that I know of, but you can say it's according to Grampa."

Chapter 11 Where did Satan come from?

That evening at dinner, Emily had another question for her grandparents.

"Where did Satan come from? Was he created by God? If so, why?"

Grampa scratched his chin for a moment, then addressed her question.

"The Bible's account in Genesis of the fall in the Garden of Eden raises a number of important questions. First among them is that of where does evil come from in a good world created by a good God?

"We must admit that the Bible does not exactly answer this question. But we must also acknowledge that the Bible does tell us many things that can help us make a reasonable attempt at an answer."

"In the book of Genesis 3:1, the Bible first mentions the serpent. Genesis 1 and 2 give no record of God creating any such animal. But several factors support the idea that God created serpents at the same time he made every other 'beast of the field.' For one thing, Genesis 3:1 tells us the serpent was '*more crafty than any other beast of the field that the LORD God had made*,' which implies that God made the serpent, just as he made the other beasts.

"The Bible tells us that the serpent approached Eve without in any way catching her by surprise. If this was the first she had ever seen the serpent, Eve would at least have been a little surprised by its presence.

"So we know that God created the serpent along with every other animal and that he pronounced it, and everything else, 'very good.' This is found in Genesis 1:31.

"What we do know is that the serpent, created good by God, tempts Adam and Eve and leads them to rebel against God. It is suggested that Satan inhabited the serpent and used it to deceive Adam and Eve. Revelation 12:9 proves that the serpent of the garden is none other than Satan himself, and he took the serpent's natural gifts and twisted them for his own evil purposes."

"I think I understand what you are telling me, Grampa," said Emily, "but where did Satan come from?"

"The Bible seems to teach that Satan is a created being who turned against God and embraced evil," Gramma responded. "Revelation 12:7–9 and Jude 6 are two important passages which indicate that Satan is an angel who is responsible for leading a group of fellow angels in rejecting God's authority. As a result, they were removed from heaven and 'thrown down' to earth, where they have now given themselves to making war against God's people.

"Hebrews 1:7 and 1:14 further suggest that

all angels are created beings God designed to serve him and his people. And according to Genesis 1:1, God existed all by himself (as the Trinity) in the beginning when He began His creative work. God alone is eternal. God alone is self-existent and the ground of all being (Exod. 3:14; Acts 17:28). Everything else proceeds from Him and is made by Him. Satan himself was once part of God's good creation."

Emily thought for a few moments, then asked, "If Satan—and every other creature—was created by God to be good, then where did evil come from?"

"Again, the Bible doesn't explicitly answer this question," said Grampa, "but it suggests a probable answer in at least two main ways.

"First, we are told in passages from Psalm 5:4–6, James 1:13, and 1 John 1:5 that God is not the creator of evil. He is pure light and good and there is no darkness or evil in him whatsoever. And if God cannot be tempted with evil, as James 1:13 says, then it follows that he cannot create it, because to create evil would in itself be evil.

"Second, evil is godlessness, unrighteousness, and everything else that is not

God. It's an anti-God attitude that sets something or someone against God. And if that's true, then all that's required for evil to exist is for creatures to exist who have the ability to choose or to reject God.

"Thus, evil can be said to have entered the world when God created the angels, one of whom chose to turn away from his Creator, set himself against God, and led as many others as he could to do the same."

"That makes sense, Grampa, but what does all this mean?" asked Emily.

"More than anything else, the problem of the origin of evil ought to remind us of how big our God really is. He is, as Paul says in Romans 11, 'unsearchable' and 'inscrutable,' and his ways are beyond our clear definition. God is far deeper than the deepest ocean and far greater than the greatness of the universe. For everything comes from Him and exists by His power and is intended for His glory. All glory to Him forever!"

"So, what you are telling me is that God did not create evil, but evil does exist in our world. And we can choose between God, who is goodness, and Satan, who is evil. Right,

Grampa?"

"Emily, you are right. This is difficult for many people to understand, and I'm glad you got it. We were involved in a Bible study just recently about this topic, so that's how I was able to answer your questions.

"Now, I think it's near your bedtime, young lady."

Emily said her good nights to her grandparents, called her parents, said her evening prayers, and headed upstairs to bed.

Chapter 12 Can good works save me?

The next morning, Emily came downstairs early to help Gramma get breakfast ready. As they gathered at the table, Emily began with a question for Grampa.

"I read in the Bible about doing good works, and Pastor Dave at church has talked about how important they are in our lives. Can we work our way into heaven? Through our good works, can we earn salvation?"

"Well, Emily, that's not how it works," Grampa replied. "We talked about that before.

Good works are very important in our walk with God, but salvation comes through grace, not works. We cannot earn a place in heaven by doing works on earth that are pleasing to God.

"Let's look at the book of Titus. Would you read Chapter 3, the first half of verse 5 for me?

"He saved us, not because of works done by us in righteousness, but according to his own mercy," Emily read.

"Good works don't save us; we are saved to do good works," stated Grampa. "Now, read what verse 9 says."

"The saying is trustworthy, and I want you to insist on these things, so that those who have believed in God may be careful to devote themselves to good works. These things are excellent and profitable for people," she read.

"But I don't go to work like Daddy does at his office. How can I do good works?"

Grampa chuckled and said, "Good works and good deeds are the same here. We don't need to have a job in order to do good works, or good deeds. You do this every day when you obey your parents and teachers. I know you help your mom and dad around the house with dishes,

58

laundry, and keeping your room in order. You were shown by example of parents who have a kind and gentle heart, and you have one, too. You are a very sweet young lady, and we hope you remain this way all your life.

"Good works include attending worship services, praying regularly, studying Scripture, being generous with our finances, being involved in a Bible study, caring for the poor, loving our neighbors, and so forth.

"God expects us to do good things, such as show love to our fellow human beings and not being cruel to others, including animals.

"On our farm, we raise many animals which supply us with food and income It is important that we take care of all our critters so they will produce for us, the same as we cultivate our crops to get the most and best produce from them.

"We have seen other farmers who do not take proper care of their animals, and they do not understand why their animals do so poorly. Their crops don't yield as much as ours, because they don't care for them.

"We need to have faith in God, and that faith reflects in our works. Some people talk as though they are faithful to God, but they don't show it. They don't have good works; therefore, their faith is defective, and they fall short of God's expectations. "

Grampa picked up his Bible and turned to the book of James.

"Would you please read James 2, verse 14-17?"

"What good is it, my brothers, if someone says he has faith but does not have works? Can that faith save him? If a brother or sister is poorly clothed and lacking in daily food, and one of you says to them, 'Go in peace, be warmed and filled,' without giving them the things needed for the body, what good is that? So also faith by itself, if it does not have works, is dead, " Emily read. "I don't quite understand this, Grampa. Can you explain it to me?"

"The Apostles and Jesus tried to tell the leaders of the Hebrews that just knowing God's word wasn't enough if they didn't act on what they read. They were not caring for the poor, the sick and the lame. They didn't share with those who were in need. They looked down on these people, and felt that they were undeserving. They refused even to associate with them. Paul and James considered these leaders dead in their faith, because their faith didn't produce good works."

"Salvation does not come from works," Gramma added. "Salvation is a free gift given by God to His faithful people. One of my favorite verses is Psalm 34:14. It reads, *'Turn away from evil and do good; seek peace and pursue it.'*

"Always ask yourself, 'Will what I'm about to do please God?' and you will be in God's graces." said Gramma.

Chapter 13 What happens to people who don't believe in Jesus?

Emily finished her breakfast and helped Gramma clear the table. Grampa was having some coffee and reading the morning paper. She sat down again and said, "I have another question, Grampa.

"If God is good and loves His creation, what becomes of those who don't believe in Jesus and accept Him as Savior?"

"The Bible is very clear about that, Emily,' said Grampa. "It says God counts all humans as worthy of heaven if we believe the truths about Jesus, which is known as the gospel. In particular, we must believe that Jesus is God in the flesh, that He died to pay the penalty for humanity's sin, was buried, rose from the grave, and ascended Heaven, where He reigns and gives salvation to all those who believe in Him. Peter outlined this message on the Day of Pentecost. Acts 2:38 tells us, '*And Peter said to them, "Repent and be baptized every one of you in the name of Jesus Christ for the forgiveness of your sins, and you will receive the gift of the Holy Spirit."*' Likewise, Paul said in 1 Corinthians 15:2 that people are saved from eternal judgment if they hold fast to this message.

"Many other Bible passages also teach that a person must believe in order to have eternal life in heaven. In every instance, this is the gospel truth: '*For God so loved the world, that He gave His only Son, that whoever believes in Him should not perish but have eternal life*' in John 3:16. In Romans 10:9, Paul tells us, '*If you confess with your mouth that Jesus is Lord and believe in your heart that God raised Him from the dead, you will be saved.*' Good deeds are required of every believer, but those good deeds are inevitable fruit of Christian faith, not a way of earning salvation . We are told this in James 2:14-26."

"Can someone who doesn't believe in the Christian God go to Heaven?" Emily asked.

"No," said Grampa. "Many may consider this bad news, but it's the best news imaginable because it opens Heaven's doors to even the worst sinners if they will only repent of their sins, are baptized and trust and accept God's Word."

"What about those who do good deeds? Can they earn their way into Heaven?"

"We discussed this before, but I need to repeat it. Some people believe that non-believers could go to Heaven if he or she just did enough good deeds and abstained from enough bad deeds. But the Bible warns that *'none is righteous, no, not one'* in Romans 3:10 and describes all humankind as *'dead in trespasses and sins'* in Ephesians 2:1. In other words, it is impossible to earn a spot in Heaven by righteous deeds because no one is good enough to do that. It would require moral perfection.

"Before Paul came to personal faith in Jesus Christ, he was a Hebrew of Hebrews a

Pharisee, a persecutor of the Christian church, which the Jews felt taught heresy, or untruths, and considered himself righteous, and, under the Hebrew law, he believed he was blameless. But in Philippians 3:2-11 he called all those things rubbish.

"Those who reject Jesus and His teachings will not receive salvation."

"Wow, Grampa, that sounds harsh!"

"Yes, you are right, but there is only one way to salvation, and that is through Jesus Christ, the Son of God.

"Now, Emily, I think I hear some chickens outside which need our attention. What do you think?"

"Be right there, Grampa," she said as she helped Gramma clear the table.

Chapter 14 Can a Christian lose their salvation?

Emily and Grampa came in for a nice lunch of fried chicken, mashed potatoes and gravy, and green beans that Gramma had prepared. Grampa said grace, and they began to eat. Emily helped herself to her favorite piece of chicken, the leg. As she ate, a puzzled look came over her face.

"Grampa, can a Christian lose their salvation?"

Grampa thought for a moment, then said, "You asked a question that I can't answer for certain. I have been struggling with this question myself for a long time. I once thought that salvation could be lost. Some Bible scholars will tell you that, yes, you can lose your salvation when you walk away from God and deny your belief in Him. Some suggest that once we are saved, we cannot be lost, but that is contradictory to what Hebrews 6:4-6 says.

"As we discussed earlier, many people believe everyone will be saved, that we are justified by death, and heaven is the next step after we die. However, God's Word certainly doesn't tell us that. Any quick and honest reading of the New Testament shows that the Apostles were convinced that nobody can go to Heaven unless they believe in Christ alone for their salvation. Many Biblical scholars believe that once we have confessed our belief in God and accepted Jesus as our savior, we cannot lose our salvation. Matthew 28 verse 20 reads, '*Teach* them to observe all that I have commanded you. And behold, I am with you always, to the end of the age.' This is a promise Jesus left us before He ascended into heaven. Also, they quote Deuteronomy 31 verse 8, 'It is the Lord who goes before you. He will be with you; He will not leave you or forsake you. Do not fear or be dismayed.'

"These verses and others in scripture indicate that once salvation is given, it cannot be lost. Their argument is strong. John 14:6 and Romans 10:9–10 all support this. Do you remember our earlier discussion?

"But other Christians do not agree with the answer to this question. People who would otherwise agree that only those who trust in Jesus will be saved have disagreed on whether those who truly believe in Christ can lose their salvation. We're talking about those who have fallen from the faith or at least from the confession of faith in Christ that they once made by rejecting God.

"Many believers have held that true Christians can lose their salvation because there are several New Testament texts that seem to indicate that this can happen. For example,

Paul's words in 1 Timothy 1:18–20 states that by rejecting the truth of Jesus, some have made a shipwreck of their faith, and they were handed over to Satan that they may learn not to blaspheme, which means insulting, showing contempt or lack of reverence for God. John 3:36 reads, '*Whoever believes in the Son has eternal life; whoever does not obey the Son shall not see life, but the wrath of God remains on him*'"

"This all makes sense, Grampa. I can see how someone can turn away from God and lose their salvation." Emily said. "So, which is it, Grampa? Can we lose salvation, or not?"

"Well, the Apostle Paul writes in his letter to the Colossians 1:21-23, '*Once you were alienated from God and were enemies in your minds because of your evil behavior. But now He has reconciled you by Christ's physical body through death to present you holy in His sight, without blemish and free from accusation—if you continue in your faith, established and firm, and do not move from the hope held out in the gospel.*'

"Based on what Paul writes here, I think the loss of your faith can lead to loss of salvation. But, I am sure of one thing; I've put my trust in God always, so I don't have to find out once it's too late. I do not know why a Christian with a strong faith in God would reject Him and all the truths and promises He represents. I also know there won't be any unbelievers in Heaven.

"Now, you wanted to put a jigsaw puzzle together. I think Gramma pulled out a good one for us all to work on. I will set up the card table and you and Gramma can work on it while I do some yard work. Okay?"

"That sounds great to me, Grampa."

Chapter 15 Why should we pray to God?

After lunch, Grampa mowed the lawn, and Emily helped him rake up some of the grass which had grown too tall. It was a warm day, and when they finished, Grampa suggested they go inside to cool down, work on their puzzle, and have an afternoon snack of milk and cookies. Emily thought that was a splendid idea. While they gathered around the table, Gramma joined them.

"What have you been reading about today, Emily?" asked Gramma.

"I was reading about when Jesus gathered with His disciples around the table, before they arrested Him. He had a prayer with His friends. But I have a question about this. Why do we pray to God? Doesn't God know what's going on in our lives?"

"Oh, prayer is a very important part of our lives here on earth, and it is a way we communicate with God," Gramma told her. "Prayer allows us to worship and praise God. It also allows us to confess our sins, which should lead to our genuine repentance. Prayer allows us to present our needs, concerns and desires to God. All of these parts of prayer involve communication with our Great Creator. He is personal, He cares for us, and He wants to commune with us through prayer. And, if Jesus felt the need for prayer, we must also know how necessary it is."

"Doesn't God already know our needs?" Emily asked.

"Yes He does, but sometimes we don't know what our needs are. We confuse needs with wants, and prayer allows God to know that we know what our needs are. Does that make sense?"

"Yes. I see what you mean. Sometimes I confuse my needs and my wants. I guess other people do that, too"

Gramma finished the border of the puzzle with a sigh of relief.

"There. That border is complete. Now to work on the sky.

"You should also know that God commanded us to pray. If we are to be obedient to Him, then prayer must be part of our life in Him. Jesus prayed because He was setting an example for us.

"Prayer is the means by which God makes some things happen. Prayer, for instance, helps others know the love of Jesus. Prayer can clear human problems out of the way in order for God to do His work. It is not that God can't work without our prayers, but that prayer is part of His plan for accomplishing His will in this world.

"In prayer, even the physically weak can become strong in the spiritual realm. As such, we can call upon God to grant us power over evil.

"Another reason to pray is because prayer is always available to us. Nothing can keep us from approaching God in prayer except our own choices. God wants us to communicate with

Him, and prayer is the best way to do this. Prayer keeps us humble before God. We do not ignore the intellect or reasons for faith, but prayer makes our experience of God real.

"When our prayer is answered, it can serve as a potential witness for those who doubt.

"Prayer not only strengthens our relationship with God, but when we pray with other believers, prayer also strengthens the bonds between fellow Christians."

"Does God always answer our prayers, Gramma?"

"Sometimes we get an answer right away, and sometimes He might take years for an answer to come. And, it all depends on what we pray for. It's the important prayers He answers, not trivial things like prayers to win a baseball game. And, we must keep in mind that sometimes God says 'No!' to our prayers. There are times when He has other plans in mind for us, and He doesn't answer prayers the way we want them to be answered.

"I know this is a lot to think about, Emily, but have I answered your questions about prayer?"

"I think I understand what you are telling

me, Gramma," Emily replied. "It is a way to speak with God and let Him know of our needs, desires, and the things we are concerned about."

"That's exactly it," said Gramma. "I think you have a good idea now why it's important to pray to God. We give Him praise for who He is, we thank Him for what He has given to us, and we share our needs, desires and concerns with Him. Can we pray to Him now?"

They bowed their heads, closed their eyes, and said a prayer to God. Emily said a prayer for her family, and gave thanks for what she had learned so far during her stay with her grandparents.

Chapter 16 What is the plan of salvation?

Later that afternoon, Emily came downstairs from her room to find Gramma.

"Gramma, I have a question for you. I was listening to my radio, and the preacher mentioned a plan of salvation. Do you know what he was talking about?"

Gramma smiled and reached for her Bible, which was laying next to her on an end table.

"Yes, dear, I know exactly what he was talking about. We talked briefly about it a few days ago, but I didn't refer to it as the plan of salvation. I keep a copy of it right inside my Bible.

"First of all, we need to be saved because we have all sinned, right? We have talked about sin earlier, so you know what this is."

"Right, Gramma. I understand the importance of being saved," Emily replied, nodding her head and sitting near Gramma on the couch.

"Good. We all do things that harm others and dishonor God. This is sin. We are all sinners; none of us is perfect.

"Now, we cannot save ourselves; only God can save us. Jesus died as the ultimate sacrifice for us, and through Him we can receive salvation. This is our first step."

"First step?" asked Emily. "You mean there is more than one step?"

"Yes, my dear. There are more," Gramma replied. "Open your Bible to the book of Hebrews, and find chapter 11, verse 6. What does it say?"

"'*And it is impossible to please God*

without faith. Anyone who wants to come to him must believe that God exists and that he rewards those who sincerely seek him.' So, our first step is to trust God and believe in Him, right?" Emily asked.

"Yes, that is what we are to do. The second thing we need to do is confess. We need to acknowledge God and accept Him as our savior, and acknowledge our sins. Let's look at Romans chapter 10. Would you read verse 9, please?"

"*'If you openly declare that Jesus is Lord and believe in your heart that God raised him from the dead, you will be saved,'*" Emily read.

"Acceptance of God and Jesus with all our heart is a very important part of salvation. Some people say the words, but do not take them seriously, and don't really accept God as their savior.

"Now, let's look at Acts chapter 3, verse 19. Would you read this, please?"

"*'Now repent of your sins and turn to God, so that your sins may be wiped away.'*"

"This is the third step; to repent of our sinful ways," said Gramma. "This means we must give up our life of sin and try to please God in everything we do. Be truthful, obey our parents, and be nice to those around us, even if we do not know or like them. This is very difficult for many people to do."

"I even have to like Jennie Smith, who picks on me?" asked Emily. "How do I do that?"

"We can start by praying for her." Gramma said. "Matthew 5:44 records Jesus as saying, *'But I say, love your enemies! Pray for those who persecute you!'* Again, this is very hard for some people to do. Hatred is a very strong emotion, and if we don't eliminate hatred from our lives, we are not pleasing God.

"Step 4 is to be baptized. Let's look at Acts 2:38."

Emily turned to Acts, and read the scripture. *"And Peter said to them, 'Repent and be baptized every one of you in the name of Jesus Christ for the forgiveness of your sins, and you will receive the gift of the Holy Spirit.'"*

"This is a step many Christians leave out. There is nothing magical about baptism, but it was extremely important to Jesus. He was baptized by John the Baptizer when He began His ministry. Jesus was sinless, but wanted to show us the way to salvation. John baptized Jesus in the river. If you think baptism isn't important, look at Jesus's last words as recorded in Matthew 28:19. Matthew says,

"*Therefore, go and make disciples of all the nations, baptizing them in the name of the Father and the Son and the Holy Spirit.*'

"This is referred to by many as 'the great commission. If baptism isn't important, why did Jesus command us to do this?"

Gramma paused for Emily to consider this question.

"Wow! It certainly must be important, Gramma!" she exclaimed.

"The final step is to live a life that honors God. Let's read what Paul wrote in the book of 1 Thessalonians 4:1-2. Would you read that, my dear?"

"*Finally, dear brothers and sisters, we urge you in the name of the Lord Jesus to live in a way that pleases God, as we have taught you. You live this way already, and we encourage you to do so even more. For you remember what we taught you by the authority of the Lord Jesus.*'"

"Paul is telling us that once we have cleaned the sin out of our lives, we must try to live as sinless as possible, and we are to confess and repent of our sins to God. Paul tells us that once we become followers of Christ, we must not revert to our old sinful lives. He says we take off the old self and put on the new self. That's what becoming a Christian is all about."

"You have given me a lot to think about, Gramma."

"Well, Emily dear, how about you think about this while you help me make a cherry pie? We can have some for desert after supper."

Chapter 17 How do I know I'm going to Heaven?

That evening, Gramma, Grampa and Emily were watching television, and enjoying cherry pie and ice cream. Suddenly, Emily turned to Gramma with a question.

"Gramma, we talked about baptism today, and I'd like to know more about it."

"Ok, Emily. I think I can explain it to you.

"Baptism signifies the death of the sinful person and a resurrection of a new person in

Christ. As you enter the water waiting to be baptized, you symbolize Jesus' death on the cross. As you are submerged, it symbolizes Jesus' burial in the tomb. As you are brought up out of the water, you symbolize Jesus' resurrection from the dead. That's what baptism is."

"If you read about John the Baptist," said Grampa, "or John the Baptizer, as some call him, you read about Jesus coming to him to be baptized. We talked some about this earlier. Jesus was sinless, but wanted to show us what to do. Some people dismiss baptism as not necessary, but why then was Jesus baptized?

"John was calling the Jewish people to confess their sins and repent through being immersed in the Jordan River. Sinless Jesus asked John to baptize Him. When we follow Him into the waters of baptism, we're publicly confessing our faith in Him."

"So, when I'm baptized, I die and am brought back to life again," Emily asked. "Grampa and I talked about this earlier today, but I don't quite understand this. It all sounds scary to die."

Gramma picked up her Bible and said,

"You don't actually physically die and come back to life again. In Romans 6:3-4 this is how the apostle Paul puts it: *'Don't you know that all of us who were baptized into Christ were baptized into his death? We were therefore buried with him through baptism into death in order that, just as Christ was raised from the dead through the glory of the Father, we too may live a new life.'* Does that help you understand this more?"

"Yes, I think so. But, does baptism save me?"

"No, Emily," said Grampa. "Baptism doesn't save you. Your salvation comes by faith alone in God. You are saved through the grace of God. Your sins are forgiven the moment you accept Christ as your savior. Baptism is your passage from the old life to the new life."

"I've heard about infants being sprinkled just after birth. Is this the same as baptism?"

"Well, dear," Gramma began, "the word baptize comes from the Greek word 'baptizo,' which means to dip, plunge, or immerse. And, baptism needs to be performed after a person is old enough to realize they are confessing sins and accepting Jesus the Christ as their savior."

"Since you are personally being baptized," Grampa added, " you can say, 'I died with Jesus, I was buried with him and now I am raised with Him to a brand new life.'"

"So this is a very important step in my life as a Christian! I think I understand now."

"Our Savior commands us to follow the examples He has set for us in all things. Matthew 28:19 says, '*Go therefore and make disciples of all the nations, baptizing them in the name of the Father and the Son and the Holy Spirit.*' Remember, we talked about this earlier today." said Gramma.

Emily thought about all this for a time, as they watched television.

"I have another question. If baptism doesn't give me salvation, how do I know I'm saved? You said I received it through God's grace, but how do I know He has given it to me?"

Grampa rubbed his chin, and then responded.

"It all starts, I guess, with sin. Sin comes into our life, and separates us from God. Sin also keeps us out of Heaven. But how can we get rid of our sins? We can't erase them or cause them to disappear. We talked about sin earlier. The only way to get rid of our sins is for someone to take them away for us. Jesus did this for us when He died on the cross. He took the punishment we deserve. '*For Christ died for sins once for all, the righteous for the unrighteous, to bring you to God*' says 1 Peter 3:18. We are saved through God's grace, a gift He freely gives us. What we have to do is accept His gift."

"Now, what must you do?" asked Gramma. "We talked about the plan of salvation. You receive God's grace from your actions, and you will be saved. This promise from God is for you: '*To all who received him, to those who believed in his name, he gave the right to become children of God*'. This is from John 1:12. Are you ready to become God's child by asking Christ to come into your life?"

"Yes I am, Gramma! I want to be a child of God!"

Gramma and Grampa both applauded and cheered. They prayed that Emily should receive, through the grace of God, the gift of salvation.

"We will call your parents," Grampa said, "and make arrangements for your baptism in the river when they come to pick you up. This is the most important decision you will ever make, as it assures your life in Eternity with God as you accept Him. May God bless you, dear Emily!"

Chapter 18 The Christmas Story

Over 2000 years ago, there was a man named King Herod. He ruled the country of Judea, now part of Israel. During this king's reign, God sent an angel by the name of Gabriel to visit a young Hebrew woman who lived in the city of Nazareth. This young girl's name was Mary, and she was engaged to marry a man named Joseph.

Gabriel said, "Peace be with you, Mary! God is pleased with you and is to bless you!"

Mary was shocked by this visitor and his message, which she did not understand.

The angel said to her, "Fear not, for God has been very kind to you. You will be with child by the Holy Spirit and soon you will give birth to a baby boy. You will name Him Jesus. He is God's Son and His kingdom will never end."

Now, Mary was very much afraid but she also trusted God.

"Let it happen as God chooses," she told the angel.

Gabriel also told Mary, "Your cousin, Elizabeth, who thought she was too old and unable to have a child, soon will be having a baby boy. God has chosen him to prepare the way for your Son, Jesus."

Mary told her family and friends goodbye, and she went to visit her cousin and her husband, Zechariah. Elizabeth was excited and pleased to see Mary, because she knew God had chosen her to be the mother of his Son. Zechariah had also been visited by an angel, who told him that Elizabeth's baby would prepare the Hebrews to welcome Jesus. Her son's name would be called John. Mary stayed with Elizabeth about three months and then returned to Nazareth and home.

Joseph was worried that Mary was expecting a baby when he found out, as their marriage had not yet taken place. He had thoughts about cancelling their wedding. But, an angel appeared to him in a dream.

"Don't be afraid to take Mary as your wife. She has been chosen by God to be the mother of

His Son. He will be named, Jesus, which means 'Savior' because he is being sent to save the people."

When Joseph awoke from this dream, he took Mary as his wife, as the angel had told him to do.

The land where Mary and Joseph lived was part of the vast Roman Empire. The Emperor Augustus decided to have a list made of all the people in the empire so he could tax them. He decreed that everyone must return to the town or city where their families originally came from, and each person must enter their names in a register (or census). Mary and Joseph traveled a long distance from Nazareth to Bethlehem, over 70 miles, because that is where Joseph's family called home. Most people walked but a few of the more well-to-do families owned a donkey to help carry what was needed for the journey. Mary's baby was due to be born soon, so it took them some time to travel the distance to Bethlehem.

They had a problem when they reached the city. Because of all the travelers coming to Bethlehem, they could not find a place to stay. Every house was full and every bed was spoken for. The only place they could find to stay was in a stable with animals. That final night of their travel, Mary gave birth to Jesus, the Son of God. It was the custom at that time to wrap all newborn babies tightly in a long cloth known as "swaddling clothes". Jesus' bed was the manger the animals used to eat their hay.

Close by, there were shepherds who looked after their sheep throughout the long night. That next morning, an angel appeared to them and the glory of God shone around them. The shepherds were very frightened, but the angel assured them that they were safe.

"Don't be afraid! I have good news for you and everyone. In Bethlehem, a Savior has been born. You may find Him lying in a manger."

Behind him, many more angels suddenly appeared, lighting up the sky. The shepherds heard these angels praising God, saying, "Glory to God in the highest, and peace on earth to everyone!"

After the angels departed, the shepherds decided to go to Bethlehem to see this Savior. They traveled to the city and found Mary, Joseph, and the baby Jesus. He was lying in a manger just as the angel had told them. When the shepherds saw Him, they told everyone what the angel had said and astonished everyone who heard the story. Soon, the shepherds returned to their sheep, and they praised God for sending his Son to be their Savior.

A brand new bright star appeared in sky, announcing the birth of the Savior. Some Wise Men in some far countries to the west saw the star and wanted to know what it meant. They were very clever men that studied the stars, possibly astrologers, and they believed from reading some ancient manuscripts that a new star would appear in the sky when a great king was born. They set out on a journey to find this new king and bring him gifts.

They followed the star into the country of Judea and when they arrived in Jerusalem they began to ask people, "Where is the child, the new King of the Jews?"

Herod, the king of Judea at this time, heard this and it angered him to think that someone else might be king. He was the king! He summoned these Wise Men to come to his court. He asked them to continue following this new star until they had found this new King.

"When you have found Him, come back

and tell me where He is, so that I might go and worship Him also."

But Herod did not tell them of his plan kill this new King.

The Wise Men followed the star to the city of Bethlehem, according to what they had read in the ancient writings. The star seemed to shine directly down upon the home where Jesus was.

The Wise Men entered the house where Joseph and Mary now lived and found the baby Jesus. They bowed down and worshiped Him. They had brought gifts which they spread before Him. These gifts consisted of gold, frankincense and myrrh. But God had warned the Wise Men in a dream not to return to Herod, so when they returned home to their countries in the East, they took a new route.

After they had gone, an angel appeared to Joseph in a dream.

"Get up," the angel told him, "and take Jesus and Mary. You must leave this country and go into Egypt. Stay there until I tell you, for Herod wants to find Jesus, and kill Him."

Joseph got up, took his family during the night, and they escaped to Egypt, where they lived until Herod died.

When the evil Herod realized that the Wise Men were not coming back, he was furious. He issued a decree that all the boys aged two or younger in Bethlehem and the surrounding area were to be killed. This way, he thought he could find and kill this new King. But Joseph and Mary had taken Jesus into Egypt, and to safety.

A few years later, Herod died. The angel appeared to Joseph once again.

"You can now get up and take your family back into Judea, for those who were trying kill Jesus are no longer alive."

Joseph believed the angel and soon took Jesus and Mary back to Israel. Upon arrival, he heard that Herod's son was now king of Judea. They went to Galilee instead of Bethlehem, and lived in their old town of Nazareth.

Chapter 19 the Crucifixion and Resurrection of Jesus

The Crucifixion

It was the beginning of the end, or a new beginning, depending upon how you understand the story. Jesus was arrested because the Jewish leaders believed He was preaching heresies. They refused to listen to Him, and did not understand what He was telling them. They brought him before Caiaphas, the high Jewish priest. With him were the teachers of the Law, the pharisees, who were His accusers. Because the high priest could not order Jesus to die, He was later brought before Pilate. Although Judas, the man who betrayed Jesus to the Jewish leaders, had repented and confessed his sin, the Jewish priests ignored him. Judas, full of pain and regret, hanged himself from a tree. Jesus appeared before the governor, Pontius Pilate, and he asked Jesus: "Are you the king of the Jews?" "You have said so," Jesus replied.

He was accused by the chief priests and elders before the governor, but He did not answer, remaining silent. Pilate asked the people if they wanted him to release the best-known criminal of those days, Barabbas, or Jesus, who was called the Christ. The people asked for Barabbas. The priests saw Jesus as an enemy and a blasphemer. They did not understand that he was the Messiah.

The Romans took Jesus away, tied Him to a whipping post, and whipped Him with 39 lashes with a whip called a "cat-o-nine-tails." This tore into His flesh and was excruciatingly painful.

Then He was taken to Golgotha, which means "the Place of the Skull". They put a crown of thorns upon His head. There Roman soldiers hung Him to a cross with nails through his hands or wrists, and His feet. Pilate had a sign put on the cross above Jesus, proclaiming Him "King of the Jews."

His cross was placed between two thieves, who were being crucified for their crimes. But Jesus was not a criminal, having done nothing wrong. He was sinless! Yet, He was insulted, despised and mocked. The day darkened. Jesus gave a great cry saying: "Eli, Eli, lema sabachthani?" (Which means: "My God, my God, why have You forsaken me?") And soon he died. One of the Roman guards thrust a spear into Jesus's side to show He was dead.

There was a great earthquake and the veil of the Hebrew Temple in Jerusalem was torn in half. Joseph of Arimathea, one of his followers, offered his tomb for burial of the body of Jesus. Since He had predicted that on the third day he would be resurrected, the chief Jewish leaders came to Pilate to ask him to seal the tomb.

"We fear that his disciples may come, steal the body, and tell the people that he has been raised from the dead," they said.

The Resurrection

At dawn on the first day of the week (Sunday), Mary Magdalene and the other Mary went to the tomb to anoint Jesus' body with herbs, which was a Jewish tradition. As they arrived, there was a great earthquake and an angel awaited for them at the tomb.

The angel said to the women, "Do not be afraid, for I know that you are looking for Jesus, who was crucified. He is not here; He has risen, just as He said. Come and see the place where

He lay. Then go quickly and tell His disciples: 'He has risen from the dead and is going ahead of you into Galilee. There you will see Him.' Now I have told you."

They hurried to tell the disciples, who did not believe them, but went to the tomb to verify what the women were telling them. They found the women to be truthful; the stone was rolled away, and the tomb was empty. Pilate had stationed two soldiers there to guard the tomb. Their lives depended upon them doing their job. The disciples could NOT have come to steal the body. Jesus had risen!

Jesus first appeared to Mary Magdalene, out of whom He had driven seven demons. She went and told those who had been with Him and who were mourning and weeping about Jesus' death. When they heard that Jesus was alive and that Mary Magdalene had seen Him, they could not believe it.

Later, Jesus appeared in a different form to two of His followers while they were walking in the country. The men returned and reported it to the rest; but they did not believe them either.

Jesus then appeared to the Eleven as they were eating; He rebuked them for their lack of faith and their stubborn refusal to believe those who had seen Him after He had risen.

"Go into all the world," He told them, "and preach the gospel to all creation. Whoever believes and is baptized will be saved, but whoever does not believe will be condemned. And these signs will accompany those who believe: In my name they will drive out demons; they will speak in new tongues; they will pick up snakes with their hands; and when they drink deadly poison, it will not hurt them at all; they will place their hands on sick people, and they will get well."

After the Lord Jesus had spoken to them, He was taken up into heaven and he sat at the right hand of God. This was forty days after Jesus had risen from the grave, and He had been seen by hundreds of people.

After the ascension, the disciples went out and preached everywhere, and the Lord worked with them and confirmed his word by the signs that accompanied it. They were able to preach the good news in everyone's language on the Day of Pentecost. Later we learn that the apostles healed believers, and Paul was bitten by a poisonous snake, and did not die. Jesus suffered like no other human being. We need to remember His sacrifice for us. And we must also remember He rose from the grave. Jesus, the Messiah, is risen!

###

Chapter 20 Important Scriptures To Know

Psalm 23 - A Psalm of David.

The Lord is my shepherd; I shall not want. He makes me lie down in green pastures. He leads me beside still waters. He restores my soul. He leads me in paths of righteousness for His name's sake. Even though I walk through the valley of the shadow of death, I will fear no evil, for you are with me; your rod and your staff, they comfort me. You prepare a table before me in the presence of my enemies; you anoint my head with oil; my cup overflows. Surely goodness and mercy shall follow me all the days of my life, and I shall dwell in the house of the Lord forever.

Matthew 5:14-16

"You are the light of the world. A city set on a hill cannot be hidden. Nor do people light a lamp and put it under a basket, but on a stand, and it gives light to all in the house. In the same way, let your light shine before others, so that they may see your good works and give glory to your Father who is in heaven."

The Ten Commandments - from Exodus 20:2-17

1. I am the LORD your God, who brought you out of the land of Egypt, out of the house of bondage. You shall have no other gods before Me.
2. You shall not make for yourself a carved

image—any likeness of anything that is in heaven above, or that is in the earth beneath, or that is in the water under the earth; you shall not bow down to them nor serve them. For I, the LORD your God, am a jealous God, visiting the iniquity of the fathers upon the children to the third and fourth generations of those who hate Me, but showing mercy to thousands, to those who love Me and keep My commandments.

3. You shall not take the name of the LORD your God in vain, for the LORD will not hold him guiltless who takes His name in vain.

4. Remember the Sabbath day, to keep it holy. Six days you shall labor and do all your work, but the seventh day is the Sabbath of the LORD your God. In it you shall do no work: you, nor your son, nor your daughter, nor your male servant, nor your female servant, nor your cattle, nor your stranger who is within your gates. For in six days the LORD made the heavens and the earth, the sea, and all that is in them, and rested the seventh day. Therefore the LORD blessed the Sabbath day and hallowed it.

5. Honor your father and your mother, that your days may be long upon the land which the LORD your God is giving you.

6. You shall not murder.

7. You shall not commit adultery.

8. You shall not steal.

9. You shall not bear false witness against your neighbor.

10. You shall not covet your neighbor's house; you shall not covet your neighbor's wife, nor his male servant, nor his female servant, nor his ox, nor his donkey, nor anything that is your neighbor's."

Mark 12:28-34 The Great Commandment

And one of the scribes came up and heard them disputing with one another, and seeing that he answered them well, asked him, "Which commandment is the most important of all?" Jesus answered, "The most important is, 'Hear, O Israel: The Lord our God, the Lord is one. And you shall love the Lord your God with all your heart and with all your soul and with all your mind and with all your strength.' The second is this: 'You shall love your neighbor as yourself.' There is no other commandment greater than these." And the scribe said to him, "You are right, Teacher. You have truly said that

*He is one, and there is no other besides Him.
And to love Him with all the heart and with all
the understanding and with all the strength, and
to love one's neighbor as oneself, is much more
than all whole burnt offerings and sacrifices."
And when Jesus saw that he answered wisely, He
said to him, "You are not far from the kingdom
of God." And after that no one dared to ask him
any more questions.*

John 3:16

*For God so loved the world, that He gave His
only Son, that whoever believes in Him should
not perish but have eternal life.*

Romans 8:28

*And we know that for those who love God all
things work together for good, for those who are
called according to his purpose.*

Proverbs 3:5-6

Trust in the Lord with all your heart, and do not lean on your own understanding. In all your ways acknowledge him, and he will make straight your paths.

Romans 12:2

Do not be conformed to this world, but be transformed by the renewal of your mind, that by testing you may discern what is the will of God, what is good and acceptable and perfect.

Ephesians 2:8-9

For by grace you have been saved through faith. And this is not your own doing; it is the gift of God, not a result of works, so that no one may boast.

1 John 1:9

If we confess our sins, He is faithful and just to forgive us our sins and to cleanse us from all unrighteousness.

Matt. 25: 34-40

Then the King will say to those on his right, 'Come, you who are blessed by my Father, inherit the kingdom prepared for you from the foundation of the world. For I was hungry and you gave me food, I was thirsty and you gave me drink, I was a stranger and you welcomed me, I was naked and you clothed me, I was sick and you visited me, I was in prison and you came to me.' Then the righteous will answer him, saying, 'Lord, when did we see you hungry and feed you, or thirsty and give you drink? And when did we see you a stranger and welcome you, or naked and clothe you? And when did we see you sick or in prison and visit you?' And the King will answer them, 'Truly, I say to you, as you did it to one of the least of these my brothers, you did it to me.'

##

A final note from the author

It is my mission in developing this book to assist you, the reader, in understanding God and what being a Christian is all about. It is my hope and prayer that this book will help readers accept Jesus as their Lord and Savior, and come to know and receive the precious gift of salvation that our Lord God has freely given us. This is **the** most important decision you will ever make in your life! May God bless you in your walk with Him!

About the author

John Mitchell is a graduate of Purdue University, is a disabled Vietnam veteran, having attained the rank of Staff Sergeant with the U. S. Air Force. He has been married for over 38 years. He retired as purchasing manager from a large machinery manufacturer after working in industrial manufacturing for over forty years. He began writing children's books after retirement, and has now published eight books and is working on his next one. He was baptized over sixty years ago, and has served as Deacon, Elder and church teacher.

John's other books

George And Smokey; A Tale of Two Cats

Nightwings The Bat

Little Bird's Big Adventure

The Tale of Mama Kitty's Tail

Uncle Bob and the pig-headed sow

Cosmonaut and Taikonaut Autographs
An Identification Guide

Something Seems Fishy (with Gary Stanford)

CPSIA information can be obtained
at www.ICGtesting.com
Printed in the USA
JSHW082132030223
37136JS00003B/12